ON MORAL PSYCHOLOGY AND MORAL PHILOSOPHY: TOWARDS A NEW THEORY OF EMOTIONS, MOTIVATIONS, AND ETHICS, USING THE INSIGHT THAT EMOTIONS PAY MORAL DEBTS

AND MORAL CREDITS OWED TO SELF AND LOVED ONES

Russell Hasan

For My Mother.

CONTENTS

INTRODUCTION

This is an essay on forgiveness, not in the religious sense, but in a purely secular meaning, as in, when one person forgives another person for something they did wrong. The primary focus is on self-forgiveness, where a person forgives themselves, a concept which this essay explains as "moral bankruptcy," using debts and credits and bankruptcy and economics and finance as a metaphor for the moral debts and moral credits that you owe to yourself and to others, that you owe it to yourself to be a good person, and you owe it to other people to be good to them, and, where you fail, you owe them a debt. The human brain evolved in such a way that humans tend to subconsciously seek to repay moral debts through the infliction of emotional pain, either inflicting emotional pain upon the self for debts owed to self (guilt), inflicting pain upon the self for debts owed to others (shame), or inflicting pain upon others for debts they owe to you (anger). This essay, despite being atheistic and secular in nature, does explore forgiveness in the context of areas that are commonly thought of as religious sins: lust, greed, pride, envy, and evil, as well as shame and guilt. The key central idea is that self-forgiveness, "moral bankruptcy," can help set you free from any guilt, shame, and anger that is holding you back in your life, and forgiveness will enable you to live a happier life, by giving you the confidence to act, and to achieve, with a greater resistance to fear of feeling guilt or shame if you fail, thereby tranquilizing fear of rejection or fear of failure or fear of disappointment. This theory of emotions will define honor, emotional maturity, self-esteem, and confidence, as well as explaining all of the seven major emotions: happiness, sadness, love, fear, guilt, shame, and anger. This book is cold, logical, no-nonsense wisdom about forgiveness, and is not mere wishy-washy empty generalities like most self-help books.

MORAL BANKRUPTCY

In The Genealogy of Morals, Friedrich Nietzsche put forward a theory of emotions which I refer to as emotional capitalism. If one of your friends or loved ones owes you a moral debt, and does not repay in kind, you may exact payment by being mean and nasty to them. If you owe them a moral debt, you can repay by being nice to them, or by letting them be mean to you. If someone owes you, you may seek their feelings and expressions of gratitude to pay the debt, or inflict emotional pain to recover your debt. Emotional capital is the debts and credits you owe, or are perceived to owe, to the people in your life.

Emotions can be explained in this way: you feel guilt if you owe a moral debt to someone else to give them your pain in order to pay off your debt. You feel shame if you owe a moral debt for failing social norms or if you owe a debt to society, again, to give your suffering to your creditor as payment. And you feel anger toward someone if they owe you a moral debt which they are not repaying, to extract what you owe from them by getting pain from them when you cause pain to them.

For example, say that you feel you have been a good employee for several years and you deserve a promotion, and your boss passed you over for a promotion and promotes someone else instead. You might get angry at your boss, because, either consciously or subconsciously, you desire to cause your boss pain equal to the moral debt that your boss owed you when he wronged you. Obviously to get angry in this way would be a great way to get fired from your job and lose your salary and ruin your life. Later it will be shown how forgiveness, implemented as moral bankruptcy and emotional maturity, would enable you to forgive your boss, and be a happy productive employee at work.

This theory takes its most interesting turn with the idea that, when you owe something to yourself and fail to obtain it, you owe to yourself a debt you cannot repay, which you must then pay to yourself by inflicting pain and punishment upon yourself: this is the theory of emotional guilt. Moving forward this essay will frequently refer to guilt as the self-inflicted pain of a debt owed to self, and refer to shame as a debt owed to others, although there are some nuances and wrinkles in these definitions. Later it will become clear that shame usually causes guilt to go with it, because you let yourself down by not being good enough for the others whom you sought to impress, and, for this reason, guilt and shame can function as one entity in reality.

From here we finally see the groundwork laid for a theory of moral bankruptcy. In legal bankruptcy, the law forces creditors to absolve the debts of the debtor, in order to give the debtor a fresh start and freedom. Absent bankruptcy it would probably be inevitable to bring back debtors prison and indentured servitude, which is a road to slavery. Moral bankruptcy operates along similar principles. Michel Foucault once hypothesized that there is an Internalized Other in each person's head whereby society conditions a person to cast society's judgment upon himself internally. To the extent that a person has a sense of social judgment, and an accounting of one's emotional capital, one acts in this capacity as bankruptcy court judge, and one then looks in the mirror and sees oneself as debtor to oneself as creditor, to the extent one failed in what one was morally obligated to give to oneself.

You were stupid in how you applied for a job, you did not try hard enough to obtain a goal, you did not put up enough of a fight to save a romance, etc. You look at yourself and declare that you are filing for moral bankruptcy. The judge then absolves all emotional debts, you are forgiven, you have absolved yourself for the sin against yourself that you had committed, and you move on with your life.

The definition of emotional maturity is explained by the theory of emotional capitalism. It is the constant forgiveness of small debts to other people in your life who have been good to you in the past. Someone annoys you with some small wrongdoing against you and you forgive them instead of seeking to recover what they now owe to you, and you forgive them in your emotions, and hold no urge nor feeling to get pain from them.

This is a sound way to do business in a capitalist economy. This is like a car dealer who pays off your loan as the cost of making the sale happen. Between two merchants who frequently do business with each other, forgiving small debts is a matter of convenience and practical necessity. Such is the definition of being emotionally mature.

In contrast, an emotional toddler is someone whose recovery of tiny debts owed to them is swift and extreme. Such people will throw a temper tantrum to make you feel bad if they feel bad and blame you in any small extent, either consciously or unconsciously. If they resent you, such as by categorizing you as the type of person from whom they blame their miserable lives, or if they feel that the type of person you are, or you specifically, have treated them unfairly, they will seek to recover what they feel owed in the most juvenile way possible.

Honor is defined as the quality of repaying and taking debts owed by you or to you according to your own internal moral ledger without needing any external pressure to be forced to do so. Honor and emotional maturity do not contradict, because an honorable man strives to repay outgoing debt (debts owed to others) whereas a mature man strives to forgive incoming debts (debts owed to him). Because you own debts owed to you, you may do as you please with them, and forgive them, and this is not theft. This is true if you owe a debt to yourself. In contrast you cannot force someone else to forgive a debt because that would be theft.

Debts can have orders of magnitude, also known as scale. A higher order debt can offset a lower order debt, for example, I owe you $50 and you owe me $5, we can cancel $5 by one debt paying off the other and now I owe you $45.

A kid may recover a lower order debt by being mean to them if the parent did something wrong, but the kid's higher order debt to the parent (being given life and love, etc.) outweighs it. The kid will not know it offset but the parent will, so the parent may think the kid wronged them and be mean to the kid to recover that lower order debt, which the kid may see as a new debt owed to them that the parent wronged them again. In this way, two people must calibrate their ledgers to each other or the result can be chaos if each feels owed debts which the other does not recognize or is unaware of.

Just as the absence of bankruptcy leads to slavery, the absence of moral bankruptcy leads to emotional slavery, whereby one person takes control of another person on account of real or perceived emotional debts so high they cannot be repaid. Such is evil and the antithesis of freedom, although one's honor may naturally seek to repay debts to the fullest extent one can.

An emotional thief is someone who seizes emotional capital without paying for it, either by intentionally failing to repay emotional debts earned in the normal course of business of social relationships, or by causing pain with no remorse, not giving what is owed on their side of the ledger. Such people are evil and have dishonor.

In addition to a ledger of what is owed to a person, we humans seem to keep a mental ledger of good and bad done to us today, what life owes us. If one person after the next after the next is mean to us, we reach and break our limit, and then throw a temper tantrum to be mean to random passersby to try to recover some of what life owes us. If life is very kind to us we feel blessed and elated to have a moral surplus, and may then be in a kind and generous mood towards strangers, repaying life for what it gave to us.

Interestingly, like men, nations and races maintain an emotional ledger, and may seek repayment of debts for wrongs or rights done 700 years ago or even older. This explains much about why war or peace exists.

Parenting is also informed. The unconditional love of a (good) parent for a child will forgive any sin in return for the joy of having a child. Also, maybe we try to protect children, not from a parental instinct, but because we feel they are too young to have done anything to deserve bad things happening to them.

An emotional debt arises between two people from their actions and exists irrespective of whether one has "passed moral judgment" upon the other. Debts exist objectively, not subjectively, much as if someone loans you $20, your debt to them exists objectively because the $20 is a real physical object in your pocket. But it must be conceded that emotions and psychology are mental attributes, although what a person does is something which physically exists in objective reality, if only as what their voice says or what their body enacts (although in other books I have argued the mind and brain are identical, I don't intend to rely upon that premise in this book). What is owed and what one believes is owed may be identical, because only honor motivates most of the emotional economy, so only what people believe is owed will ever be paid, and a debt is not fully real unless we expect to collect on it somehow.

What is owed is based on the context of what you know. For example, if you know X, and because of X Jane owes you a debt, so Jane goes out of her way to be nice to you, and then you learn that X was never really true, then you now owe Jane a debt equal to what she paid you, or potentially greater if the ignorance was your own fault.

This has applications to Objectivism and Libertarianism. Objectivism is a cruel, strict master, which calls upon a person to be rational 24 hours a day, 7 days a week, with any intentional act of unreason deemed as black, putrid evil. Objectivism as ethics is to some extent a form of Perfectionism, and you are expected to be a smart person and achieve the very best that your ability could have made possible. That is a tough standard to maintain.

Moral bankruptcy, if viewed as rational, can play an important role in an Objectivist's moral life.

In libertarian political philosophy, moral bankruptcy forms a basis for "real" bankruptcy, legal bankruptcy, absent which some might view it as a debtor immorally stealing what is owed to, and owned by, a creditor. Some libertarians view bankruptcy as theft. But it is a natural part of human existence. It also justifies the libertarian darling called jury nullification: if a jury knows there is guilt under the facts and the law, but feels the accused should rightfully be forgiven, then they may vote to acquit.

The theory of emotional capitalism and moral bankruptcy can play an important role in the emotional health of Objectivists and libertarians, and everyone else, too.

GREED AND LUST: SINS, OR VIRTUES?

Let us begin with definitions and axioms, and then see where logical deduction leads.
Assume that a human being is an animal which speaks and thinks. The human as animal is body. The human as thinking entity is mind. The human as one who speaks is soul (personality, identity).
Let us assume that one human can be sexually attracted to another human because of one or more of three traits: body, mind and soul.
Define love of the body as animal love.
Define love of the soul as Platonic love.
Define love of the mind as Randian love.
We can immediately deduce that each of these three types of love possess fatal flaws. Animal love lowers oneself to a capacity one shares in common with animals and is not distinctly human. As such it lacks our highest capacity as humans. It is our basest and most disgusting nature. While the pleasure of the body is actualized, the mind and soul, our distinctly

human nature and higher capacity, are ignored.

But Platonic love denies the existence of lust and the physical world. As such, it may engender mutual esteem, but not true love, since it creates regard but not sexual desire. Lust without love should not exist, but love without lust cannot exist. Platonic love shares all the faults of Plato: seek to deny the physical world, and you will repress and deny reality, and then reality itself will undermine you and condemn you to frustration.

Then there is Randian love. Ayn Rand lived this is her relationship with Nathanial Branden: she believed that one person's love of another person's mind, with no regard for liking the other person's personality and with no lust for them physically, that mere shared intellectual values and having in common a philosophy, could form the basis for love. Randian love leads to the repression of both body and soul: you love the mind, but do not like the personality and are not attracted to the body. Then your repressed desires will eventually explode, as when the Rand-Branden affair ended with fireworks.

A form of love exists which shares none of the above flaws, which we may term Aristotelian love. Aristotelian love calls upon each person to find a ratio of body to mind to soul which is the correct expression of what they want in a lover, and to then seek that. This can be expressed as a percentage. For example, a person may care 20% about body, 10% about mind, and 70% about soul. Or a person may care 60% about body, 15% about mind, and 25% about soul.

The aspect from Aristotle is the Golden Mean: you do not want to choose too much or too little, you want just the right amount, and your correct ratio is unique to you as an individual. Too much body and you are a mere animal. Too much soul and you are a mere ghost. Too much mind and you become a mere brain without genitals.

There may be feelings of guilt if one hews to an extreme and away from the Golden Mean, as, if, for example, one cares 96% about body, 2% about mind, and 2% soul. But this is a personal choice and it would be difficult to prove that you were objectively incorrect (or to prove that you are correct). What you desire is an expression of who you are, and the only wise guidelines are "know thyself" and "to thine own self be true."

Also, for love, what each person wants must match with what the other person has. If you care about soul and someone has a great personality and sense of humor and is friendly and loving, they might be perfect for you, but if what they love is mind and, let us say, you lack a college education and are coarse and unrefined, they will not want you. What someone is and what they want have no correlation: a person may have a great body yet desire a boyfriend with a great soul, or they may have a great body and crave only another great body for pleasure, or they may have a great body and care 33% about each if the three attributes.

In true love, if and when such a thing exists, you, what qualities you possess, will satisfy all or most of what your partner seeks and vice versa. And, in reality, there is an added even deeper level of complexity, because people often feel guilty about their desires or are confused by them and so will be dishonest and lie about what they really want, making it even harder to win a good match and find real love, since you will know if you love them but might find it hard to tell if you are what they truly desire.

Something similar may be said of greed. Greed is the love of money, but it may be subcategorized into three types for analysis.

Getting money is the love of acquiring money, and is really the joy of spending money, of consuming value. We may call this selfish greed.

Making money is the joy one takes in the act of creating value, the pride that a maker has in the act of making something good, or the pride one takes in a job well done. We may call this proud greed.

Then, albeit more rarely, there is what may be termed economist's greed, which is the desire to plug into the economy and do one's job and perform one's role for the good of the economy, on account of the various economic theories which prove that it is a net benefit to society when the individual makes money. Economist's greed is honorable greed, the desire to do the work to pay all the other people in the economy who make the stuff you use, by making stuff for them to buy.

Selfish greed taken to an extreme will inspire one to theft or fraud or unethical behavior to maximize the amount of money one has. The rich people who engage exclusively in selfish greed may rightly be termed the evil rich, and there is no shortage of scams or government-enabled graft and corruption by the evil rich.

But proud greed to too great an extreme ignores the whole point of money, which is the joy of spending it and experiencing the pleasure it buys. Someone with too much proud greed might be a workaholic and work excessively, spending too much time making things instead of spending time with his family or enjoying a hobby, for example.

Economist's greed taken to an extreme can devolve into a belief, even among capitalists, that society is more important than the individual. A lot of actual economics professors are capitalists who believe this, but it undermines the moral foundation of capitalism, which is individualism. People may want to do their duty to society by working their job, but ignore their own legitimate needs for joy and pleasure.

As with lust, in greed one should discover a ratio between selfish greed, proud greed, and economist's greed, by which one avoids being evil while still selfishly enjoying life. For example, one may be motivated 75% by selfish greed, 20% by proud greed, and 5% by economic greed. Or, if one really loves one's job, and does not enjoy shopping much, one may be motivated 50% by proud greed, 30% by selfish greed, and 20% by economic greed.

One final point on the topic of lust: if lust is not a sin, then being gay/lesbian/LGBT is not a sin, and every legitimate non-criminal sexual desire/fetish is not a sin, for the same reason. However things like pedophilia and bestiality are evil, because they defy human nature and the role and purpose of sexuality, which is sex and love with consenting adults. Children and animals lack human sexual capacity physically, so human nature could not have intended them subjects of sex.

This concludes my account of lust and greed as analyzed by analytical logic with special reference to Aristotle's ethical theory of the Golden Mean.

ENVY: KEEPING SCORE

Men can compare themselves to others and fall short in many ways. One can measure and compare:
Health,
Beauty,
Wealth,
Charisma,
Intelligence,
Luck,
Strength.
One can also compare accomplishments:
Family,
Friends,
Lovers,
Children,
Career,
Skills,
Education,
Amount of joy consumed,
Amount of money made,
Amount of joy your actions enabled other people to have the freedom to consume (social libertarian

political activism), and
Amount of money your actions helped other people be free to make (economic libertarian political activism).
Because technically speaking a human should be good in every area, but in reality no one has the resources to pay the cost to achieve at a high level in literally every area, you will probably always envy at least one or more other people, if only because they chose to spend their time on an area where you spent far fewer resources and so in that area you achieved far less than they.
One might think then that wisdom lies in achieving the goals best suited to your personality and desires, for example, is your highest value becoming a doctor, or finding true love, or going on lots of vacations — because you have finite discreet limited "life resources" to spend (time and money being the big two) so you can't have everything. But in practice this wisdom can be difficult — you want to be a doctor with a love life who takes long vacations, and if you choose one you will envy everyone who chose the other two, intimately knowing the flaws of your choice but seeing only the virtues of theirs.
A Buddhist might tell you to renounce the goal of achievement. A conservative, or a strict parent, might say you had better fucking achieve or else. Neither path will make the pain of failing to achieve hurt any less.
Wisdom dictates a different path: try your best to achieve but forgive yourself if you fail. Prioritize

your goals and spend resources accordingly, mindful that, as Rand said, subjugating a lesser value to a greater one is not a sacrifice, but vice versa is (and see her essay on this topic, in The Virtue of Selfishness).

To paraphrase Nietzsche: esteeming the greatness of the achievements of other men enables us to hold the achievement of our own dreams a safe distance away from ourselves. He also might have said, or should have said: we are all of us human, all too human, and therefore must either move above our humanity or else forgive ourselves for being human.

It is also instructive to study self-esteem, in light of Rand's The Fountainhead. Take sex, for example, with a focus on what is known as "body image problems." There are those who feel that if you are hot then you deserve to have sex and are worthy (really, that you deserve to be loved) and, if you are not hot, you don't. But being hot does not correlate with deserving to have sex, only, in a practical sense, for some people it has some small impact on the game of chance of getting lucky, and no more. Self-esteem is what correlates with deserving to have sex.

We can distinguish two things: a source of self-esteem, which can be attacked but can never truly be destroyed, and the pretense of self-esteem, which can be taken away. These two things can exist for any given purpose, for example, hotness is a pretense of self-esteem for the purpose of having sex, and can be taken away (if a man says "you look fat" to a woman or to a gay man, for example). But if, for example, the source of your self-esteem for dating is confidence, that cannot be destroyed, and a woman's rejecting you may test it but will not crumble it.

A body image problem arises if your pretense at self-esteem really is based on looks and you are plausibly critical of your own hotness. As Rand artistically rendered in The Fountainhead, pull out the foundation of self-esteem and the soul collapses: this is what Toohey does to Peter Keating, and what Dominique tries and fails to do to Roark.

One can have a source or pretense of self-esteem for any purpose: career, job skills, a hobby, a friendship, your religion, your favorite author or favorite music, any facet of your identity, and it can always be attacked or challenged by other people or events or even by new facts, but self-forgiveness is a very useful tool for repairing it or fortifying it. For example, forgive and accept your body and then fret no more over it.

The basic premise of being fat-shamed is that you owe it to other people to be perfect for them so if you're not then you don't deserve to be loved. In reality there is no objective rational reason why you would owe perfection to others or need it to achieve the relatively mundane social status of love and acceptance. You deserve to be loved, you deserve to have the boyfriend or girlfriend or wife or husband of your dreams, and you deserve to have sex at will. Every good human being does.

The only obstacle is that men can use low self-esteem to exploit and control women, which is also an LGBT problem as one gay man can do this to another, much as Toohey manipulates Keating because Keating's pretense of self-esteem as an architect arises from social approval (Toohey's art criticism as the voice of society), and so there are systemic structural elements in our social existence which enable attacks against our self-esteem at any time. Adults and "normal" people are less vulnerable — unless it is their sense of normalcy itself which gets attacked.

While one is forgiving oneself for being less than perfect in a romantic context, it is also wise to forgive one's boyfriend or girlfriend or wife or husband for being less than perfect, although it is a personal decision how much is too much to forgive and when to walk away. Generally, flaws and faults should be forgiven, and such forgiveness and emotional maturity is necessary to have a healthy relationship, but pure evil should not be forgiven.

If confidence is a source of self-esteem whereas body image is not, and is a mere pretense, it may be asked how one achieves confidence. Roark in The Fountainhead is illustrative. He is a good architect, and he knows that he is a good architect. This is true even while at times in the novel everyone else is saying he is a bad architect.

You are a good person, and therefore you deserve to be loved, and your knowledge should always match the truth about objective reality, so you should know that you are a good person, and then you should know that you deserve to be loved, because these facts are true. You really are a good person, and you really do deserve to be loved. This in a sense is pride, and, in that sense, pride is a virtue, not a sin, and pride is the antidote to low self-esteem.

FORGIVENESS OF EVIL

We must ask: what if you commit a truly evil act? Is your own forgiveness enough? Or do you need God's? Or your victim's?

We must begin by asking: why did you do it? Did bad luck, circumstance, or a villain, drive you and pressure you to do it? Was it a necessary evil brought about by desperate times or an emergency? Where there is no freely chosen decision to act, there is no volitional free will so there can be no blameworthy nor culpable status.

But what if you commit the most evil sin? What if you fundamentally betray a friend, a family member, or, as I believe the most evil sin to be, what if you betray yourself and violate your integrity as an ethical human being?

What if you sell your soul, metaphorically, trading your moral righteousness and integrity to evil in return for what you want: money, power, sex, an easy way to gain success without doing hard work, or a sense of self esteem arising from how society sees you when you conform and betray who you really are by pretending to be someone else, or other vices like these? What if you looked the other way while your friend or your boss committed a crime? What if you fall into a life of crime yourself? What if you betray a friend and have an affair with his wife and lie to him repeatedly about it? Even worse crimes than these can also exist, especially in times of war or with political corruption. Even good men can be tempted to evil.

The great appeal of The Fountainhead (which nobody realizes) is that Ayn Rand addresses this. Peter Keating and Wynand both sin against Roark, but Wynand is forgiven. In the novel, climaxing at the end, Peter Keating sells his soul to Toohey for power and the pretense of self-esteem. Peter Keating gets his sense of self-esteem from how society views him, making him into the slave of social critic Ellsworth Toohey, who represents (and controls) the voice of society. Here I explore Keating's actual black sin of evil, betraying his friend and the voice of any trace of integrity left in his life, Roark, to Toohey, not even for any tangible profit but because Toohey has become his master and he has no self-respect left with which to resist the command of society for obedience.

Rand was cognizant of this betrayal as sin, and as Keating destroying his own soul, a long, drawn-out process which begins with his letting his mother pressure him to become an architect when he really wants to be an artist, grows when he abandoned the woman he loves to marry his boss's daughter to gain social status at work and in the eyes of the architecture professional, and culminates in handing evidence that Roark bombed Cortland Homes to Toohey, which Toohey wants to use to send Roark to jail, to break his spirit by force because no amount of social pressure or stigma has succeeded in getting Roark to contradict himself and renounce or sacrifice his soul to gain Toohey's (society's) favor. There is a point in the famous Toohey speech at the end of The Fountainhead where Toohey explicitly says that Keating sold his soul to him.

Rand even acknowledged this tongue in cheek where Toohey says to Peter Keating "ever read Faust?" (a German play where the main character Faust makes a deal with the devil Mephistopheles) when Keating hands him the contract that Keating and Roark signed for Roark to build Cortland Homes while Keating takes all the credit and praise for it, which Toohey needs as evidence in the courtroom trial against Roark, whereby Keating sells Roark to Toohey.

The scene much earlier in The Fountainhead where Toohey comments upon the Biblical verse "what should it profit a man, if he gaineth the world, but loseth his own soul?" (Mark 8:36), with Toohey replying "then to be truly rich one should collect souls?" is Rand's sense of humor about this issue of Keating selling his soul to the devil. In Ayn Rand's lectures on writing fiction she once said "nothing in my novels is accidental," so it is open season for us to read these religious interpretations into little details in The Fountainhead.

Wynand, too, betrays his own inner integrity, succumbs to pressure, and sells Roark to the masses to save his newspaper, at the end of the novel, again, for money, power, and the pretense of self-esteem that having built a newspaper empire makes his life meaningful. Toohey finds what Wynand built his self-esteem upon, the newspaper, takes control of it, and thereby breaks Wynand, much as he breaks Keating through his self-esteem depending on what other people think of his career and social status as an architect. This act, to betray your integrity in return for trivial sham rewards, is what I regard as the blackest sin.

But Roark forgives Wynand. Wynand in the end cannot forgive himself but as one final gesture lets Roark build the Wynand Building. He says to Roark, in the most poignant scene at the very end of the novel, "build it as a monument to that spirit which is yours . . . and could have been mine," which sums up the quest for integrity and speaks to his overwhelming sense of guilt for having betrayed Roark and for having betrayed and defiled the good in him (his friendship with Roark) in service to evil (his newspaper, the stupid masses who read it, and Toohey who controls them). But Roark forgives him and builds the building.

I think there are two lessons. If you commit the blackest sin, betraying your integrity, selling your soul to the devil, there is no external elements to this crime, it is merely your choice, so if you repent, and if you are a good person, you can forgive yourself. You control what is in you. Your moral status, whether you are good or evil, is within your control.

Second, Keating simply is evil, and Wynand just is good, it is what they are, you are what you are and your choices and actions can't ever truly change your soul. If you are a good person, that will be with you always, and any crime to which you are driven, hands stained red with blood by ill fate, cannot change what you are. If there is still goodness in your soul, if you still see the light, if you know the difference between right and wrong, this is a sufficient basis to forgive yourself, spell out your sentence of penance for you to punish yourself, repent, pick yourself up and then move on. Were you truly evil you would know only the darkness, so if you can still see light, this is proof that you have a rational basis to deserve to forgive yourself.

This is if the person you betrayed is yourself. If instead you stabbed someone else in the back, if someone died for you to live, then, in moral capitalism, you owe it to the world to save someone, or to save as many people as whose lives you ruined. This explains why religions based on guilt are so often missionary religions. Even in this case, one can earn the repayment of debts owed. And wrapped around this entire analysis stands moral bankruptcy if you have the balls to absolve punishment for a sin as black as night. Even if you hurt others, the moral injury is a wound to your own soul, which you own, and thereby you own the debt and have the legal right to forgive it.

At no point in this exposition has it become apparent that you have any need for God or religion. Yours can be a Do It Yourself forgiveness of sins. You do not need God's forgiveness because your own forgiveness is what matters, and is the moral reflection of your soul, or your moral self-worth.

What if your crime has an external victim whom your actions have wronged? When you hurt someone, you sin against three beings: your own soul as your capacity to be good and the corresponding debt you owe to yourself to be the best you that you can be, your victim equal to the emotional capital (money and/or joy) which hurting them has robbed them of, and also you sin against society, the brotherhood of all men, our great human undertaking to build a world where we help each other to be as happy as possible.

The law exacts the payment of moral debts owed to society (by fines or jail, the quintessential Nietzsche paradigm of causing pain to repay a debt from pain wrongfully caused), and this essay does not examine the laws as such, so I will not explore that area. You repay the debt to yourself and the debt to your victim with guilt, unless you forgive yourself, and unless you beg for and are granted forgiveness by your victim, in which you will no longer regard yourself as owing him your guilt. In a worst case scenario, if you are being crushed by guilt and depression, you can file for double moral bankruptcy: forgive yourself for your sin against your own soul, and forgive yourself for failure to obtain your victim's formal declaration of his forgiving you.

Ultimately if you repent with sincerity then there must still be good in you, which is a sufficient basis to "save your soul," pick up the pieces and try to put your life back together and be a good person from now on, and forgive yourself for having done evil.

People's emotions tend to believe what other people say they owe, children especially so because they don't know any better and lack a frame of reference from which to doubt. Social capitalism relies upon external validation, and children and teens do so a lot, although adults do also, to a degree inverse to their emotional maturity.

Social capitalism is emotional capitalism as it relates to, and impacts, social interaction with your peers. Your moral ledger (your mental sense of debts and credits owed) guides how you behave towards others. How others treat you, and what they say to you, is external validation or contradiction, feedback which your emotions use to calibrate the accuracy of your ledger.

For someone who was abused or bullied, as a child or teen or as an adult, the bully is essentially telling you that you don't deserve to be happy, that you don't deserve to live, and your emotions will read that as external feedback. Your emotions can be tricked into thinking you have sinned and exact payment as guilt or self-inflicted punishment. Here the act of self-forgiveness will clear the emotional fraud off the ledger. You are not, and are never, to blame for being bullied or abused, because bullying and abuse are evil by nature and so will always reflect an unjust account of debts or credits owed.

Taken to an extreme, honor combined with guilt may lead to an act of suicide, because the person seeks to repay whatever debt they feel they owe by literally giving their life to their moral creditor, but this is irrationality, and filing for moral bankruptcy is always what such a person should do instead.

At the point of death, one can no longer be good nor do good, so suicide arising from a moral basis of extreme guilt is a contradiction: one tries to do the right thing by destroying one's own moral capacity. Moreover no good creditor would ask that as repayment, so you should not ask that of yourself, and if others do then they are evil and their evilness toward you must offset whatever you think you owe them, and they can hold no moral claim upon you.

Guilt can be crippling but here the wisdom of Rand and Nietzsche is that you must have the stoic discipline for your reason to control your emotions and reach into your soul and turn off the feelings that are not objectively warranted by what you really owe to yourself or to others in the long-term.

When someone dies, we pray that they will forgive us for what we did to them in life, and we also forgive them for whatever they owed us, because the relationship is over so it is time to close the ledger and reconcile all debits and credits. Usually we feel that we treated them unfairly and were too miserly and stingy and immature, which we know only when it is too late to correct, because we were greedy and were not forced to undertake an audit until now. If, after we reconcile the ledger, we find that we owe the dead a debt which we will now never be able to repay, then we hold and cherish our memory of them for the rest of our lives, to try to repay our debt. We feel sadness to pay to the dead what we owe them, by giving them our pain (our grief), and also as a signal to our friends and loved ones to request support and comfort in any amount that our friends owe to us or are willing to lend us.

HUMAN MOTIVATIONS

Some men give to charity to seek penance for the sin of greed, to atone for being rich. That is charity from shame. Others give to charity out of an overflowing abundance of joy, that they are so happy and prosperous that they want everyone else to share their joy too. While the result is identical from the point of view of the recipient, shame is evil, and joy is good.

Our reaction to perfection is similar. Some of us, if we see someone with a perfect body or a perfect personality, immediately feel that they deserve to be loved, which reminds us that we ourselves are less than perfect, and then we feel we don't deserve love, and are sad. In times like these we must instantly forgive ourselves for being less than perfect and move on.

Other types of people, seeing someone who seems perfect, will simply feel glad for them, and share in their happiness, because they have self-esteem and confidence, and the perfection of others does not challenge and call into question their own worth.

That is the type of person who can give to charity because they are so happy and proud that their joy overflows and spills over to give to others.

The perfection of others as a challenge to our own sense of self-worth relates to a similar syndrome in all social interaction: the fear of rejection. If we "bare our soul" to someone else, if we assert not merely a minor detail about ourselves but something essential to our identity, of if we seek to share something personal and deep and meaningful with someone, we expose ourselves to rejection and make ourselves vulnerable. If you are to do so, you must be prepared to instantly forgive yourself for not having been good enough for the other person in the event that they criticize or attack your self-esteem.

Two types of people can face opportunities for rejection with other people without fear: those who are so confident that they don't expect to be rejected, and those who know that if they were rejected they would forgive themselves immediately and completely for it, and know how to do so.

Obviously it goes without saying that you owe it to yourself to act for the sake of the best within you and to thereby actualize your highest potential for joy and happiness. To actualize your highest potential is to act for the sake of the best within you. In Objectivism (from a certain point of view) your soul, your highest potential, and the best within you, are the same thing. To be good, and to be happy, you must live life to the fullest with no regrets — or with regrets that you can find it within yourself to forgive yourself for. Failure to do so is the ultimate sin, for which you will need your own forgiveness, if at the end of the day you want to be able to look in the mirror.

POLITICAL MOTIVATIONS

The inflicting of pain in order to obtain payment for an owed debt may be referred to as retribution, justice, or revenge. Such is the motive of many voters and political activists. For example, someone sees a forest get destroyed, then becomes an environmental activist to get revenge against polluters on behalf of the trees. Or someone is denied an employee benefit by her boss and then votes for a pro-labor leftist politician to get revenge against big business. Or a man sees a picture of an aborted fetus and becomes a pro-life activist to get revenge equal to the loss suffered by the fetus which he feels is now a debt owed by the pro-choice movement that created the freedom for it to happen. But in politics, as in social reality, there can be an equivalent of emotional maturity, which in this context we might name policy maturity. A higher order debt cancels out a lower order debt by offsetting the amount owed. Just having a job at all may be so important to long-term survival that the employee owes more to the employer for creating the job than the amount lost on a denial of requested benefits. Big business, by making the money that enables a society to be prosperous, might pay for conservation efforts which otherwise the human race could not afford — after all, dirty energy is cheap and clean energy is expensive, so if we couldn't afford to pay for it we would burn more coal and oil. The debt a fetus owes to its mother for existing probably exceeds any debt the mother would owe to the fetus as an obligation to be pregnant with it and give birth to it, or, at the very least, the debt of fetus to mother equals what mother owes fetus so the two debts would offset and leave a net zero.

Generally, emotional irrational thinking among voters is the equivalent of being an emotional toddler in social reality while logical rational thinking and seeing the big picture enables policy maturity.

One final point is that misattribution and misdirection may be present as well: you feel that one individual injured you and owes you an unpaid debt so you seek retribution by voting for a politician who will punish the group or category of people to whom your debtor belongs — a race, by voting for a racist politician, for example. This is obviously irrational and insane, because other people are not morally responsible for what one person has done so you should not punish a race for a debt owed by an individual. But in politics many voters behave irrationally and lack maturity.

Men give their votes to social justice crusade politicians to pay wronged groups of people for what you feel you as a member of society owe to them, so that the government will pay off your moral debt for you. You may also vote for a particular politician if you feel that he personally helped you, either individually or by aiding a group or class you belong to, because you owe a moral debt to them. And then there are voters who feel blessed to live in a good society and feel it is a repayment of what one owes for being given this blessing to vote for a politician who will fight for goodness and virtue and truth and justice. Libertarian policy is generally superior to socialism, but such a basis for votes in emotional capitalism are usually based on how you feel about the politician, not how you feel emotionally about his policy.

There are many ways in which forgiveness and sin play out in politics. People see a group or class of citizens whom they feel have been wronged, and then vote for a government to right that wrong, to give those people what they are owed, which is called fairness and justice and is really the repayment of debts owed so that both sides of the ledger even out. But the libertarian point of view is that, if you feel a wrong has been done, it is your job, not the government's job, to help fix it, spending your own money, not other people's money, because you have the right to spend money you own but lack the right to take money from others even for a good cause.

But what if by yourself you don't have enough money to fix it, so collectively pooling money is necessary for justice? Then persuade large numbers of others to freely and voluntarily donate to your charity, don't force them to give money against their will by government tax and spend. The money you would owe to the taxpayers you robbed would equal any justice of debt repaid to an oppressed class.

It is not the job of government to forgive us for being human and for making mistakes, by removing our freedom to make mistakes and replacing it with a dictator's control. Instead, forgive yourself by doing the work necessary to get what you want, and then you will obtain it, and the only thing that could stop you then is bad luck, for which you should feel no blame. I am not a Christian but believe strongly in this: "Ask and ye shall be given, Seek and ye shall find, Knock and the door shall open." (Matthew 7:7). If you want money, go get it. If you want a job, find one. If you don't choose to get what you want, that is a sin, but government can't fix that, that is something only you can do. If you hit rock bottom, are poor or homeless, file for moral bankruptcy, stop feeling sorry for yourself and start over.

There are also those who feel they are not worthy to be happy and lack self-esteem and feel they don't deserve to live, so embrace any dictatorship that will punish them to give them what they feel they are morally owed: suffering, a total lack of responsibility for making the decisions which control your own fate, and, eventually, death. These people need to forgive themselves and seek a sense of self-worth, but, absent that, we the living must not allow ourselves to be dragged into Hell by those who are half dead already.

When the government has total control, regardless of whether politicians are good or evil, the citizens have no free will, hence cannot make mistakes, hence can do nothing for which they need to be forgiven. But it is also true that, lacking free will, they can commit no blessings nor virtues and do nothing that is right and good, having no ability to make any decision or ethical choice of right or wrong at all. Such a scenario is manifestly repugnant to the moral lives of human beings.

With respect to politics, it is also wise to remember this Bible verse: "All those who sin are a slave of sin." (John 8:34). If you sacrifice your moral integrity, you will very quickly find yourself under the control of evil men, and, ultimately, of evil politicians or dictators. The evil in you will seek out the evil in them, and, having turned to the darkness, you will not have the light within you to shine at them to drive them away. If someone else controls your self-esteem then they can destroy you, so your soul becomes their slave. Although I am a Libertarian, I want to point out that any type of politician may seek to exploit you: the socialists, liberals, conservatives, and, if there were any, libertarians. Remember with warning what Toohey says: "It's the soul, Peter, the soul, not whips or swords or fire or guns. ... The soul, Peter, is that which can't be ruled. It must be broken. … You won't need a whip — he'll bring it to you and ask to be whipped."

MORAL ECONOMICS

Let me point out that, in Atlas Shrugged, in the scene where James Taggart accuses Cherryl of having a shopkeeper's morality and she accuses him of seeking the unearned in spirit, Rand gets at her closest to articulating an idea that pervades Atlas Shrugged, the idea that moral value and economic value is equivalent, that morality and finance are comparable. Esteem is to be paid for by being a good person, success is to be paid for by doing the right thing ethically. Moral value as a human is to be earned by doing the hard work of living an ethical life. And you earn your social and romantic relationships by doing the work to make the relationship work and to give the other person what they enjoy in return for you getting what makes you happy.

Emotions are like money, in this way: money is a loan, in that the owner of a $1 bill is owed $1 worth of value; the dollar bill is a promissory note that the economy is to give back $1 worth of value if the owner hands over the dollar bill to the economy. An emotion is a record of money on your moral ledger; for example, if you love someone, then you owe them your devotion because they have already paid you for it by being the person you are in love with or by loving you. Your emotions tell you what you owe and are owed, just as a $10 bill tells the economy that it owes you $10 worth of value, $10 worth of goods and services to consume, because you lent the economy an hour of labor at your job that paid you a salary of $10/hour.

Values — moral values — can be earned, stolen, bought, sold, traded, and, yes, loaned or borrowed or repaid. The thesis of this paper is to take this concept seriously, and then understand how bankruptcy works in a moral economic system. Much as the finance system and capitalism in the USA could not function absent bankruptcy law to govern debtors and creditors in the event of insolvency, so too moral capitalism cannot exist absent a formalized system of forgiveness. It is then a logical analysis of human nature to say that our emotions evolved as our ledger in moral capitalism, telling our conscious minds to take what we are owed and give back where we owe debts.

Feelings and emotions, in this way, are vital to ethics, and it is also worth noting that emotions are not inherently irrational and illogical as such, and play an important role in a rational life. However your subconscious mind may have a different belief about your debts than your conscious mind, which is where reason and emotions might conflict, and you must reconcile how you feel with what you believe. Do not assume that your reason is correct and your emotions incorrect, nor vice versa, but undertake a substantial detailed analysis to discover the truth.

It might be asked why the human brain tends to subconsciously dish out pain (or pleasure, as discussed in the next chapter) to repay moral debts and credits. My position is that this is simply a feature of human evolution, although one might see it as a moral fact, that your brain tries to give you what you deserve. Humans seem to have evolved from primates who survived as pack or tribe animals. They formed tribes, and families within those tribes, which would have required a precise calibration of how to assign help to each other, as for sharing food, or hunting, etc., and who owed what to whom. Our biological ancestors were "social animals," to take a phrase from Aristotle which is probably better translated as "social by nature." As such, not only our reason and mind, but also our social reactions, are highly evolved. I see moral economics as an aspect of the human brain arising from our evolution as social animals.

Here I will share a happy thought. So you sinned. You let yourself down. You failed. Your wife and kids are mad at you. You're not the greatest person at your job. You wanted to do something very much but lacked the courage or the will to do it. You reasoned that you should pursue a path but let irrational fears talk you out of it. Or something similar. You sinned against your own soul by failing to act for the sake of the best within you. Or you sinned against someone else. You didn't buy the best gift for your girlfriend because you didn't want to spend the money. You were not supportive of a friend in a time of need because it was too difficult and stressful. You were a doctor and made the wrong decision and a patient died, or you were a soldier in a war and one of the other soldiers died in combat to rescue you and you survived but they died.

You feel guilt, to make yourself suffer in order to repay the debt that you cannot otherwise repay: a debt you owe to yourself, or to someone else. For the doctor who owes life to the dead or the soldier with survivor's guilt, in their emotional capitalism ledger they may feel the need to hurt themselves with guilt in an amount equal to the value of life itself, because they feel they owe a life to the person who died.

But that's humanity. That's being human. You sinned. So what else is new? We all fail. Everyone does. Forgive yourself. Use moral bankruptcy. You are a good, special, wonderful person. You still deserve to be happy. Repeat that: you deserve to be happy.

You're a good person and you deserve to be happy. And you deserve to love, and you deserve to be loved. Never forget that. They say "forgive and forget." Yes, forgive. But never forget that you deserve to be happy.

CONCLUSION

This essay has succeeded in explaining a theory of emotions, motivations, and ethics, which explained everything that it set out to explain. Guilt and shame and anger have been explained by reference to the infliction of emotional pain to repay, or retake, pain as payment for moral debts that are owed. Honor was explained as the willingness to repay the moral debts that you owe to others without being forced to do so, while emotional maturity was explained as a tendency towards forgiveness of small debts on a daily basis. Moral bankruptcy was presented as the paradigm for self-forgiveness, using finance and economics as a metaphor for moral economics.

However, happiness, love, sadness and fear have not yet been discussed. Just as the human brain inflicts pain upon someone in order to be repaid for a moral debt that they owe, so, too, the human brain evolved to feel pleasure as payment for moral credits that are owed to it. So your brain rewards you for being a good person, to self or others, with happiness, literally, with emotional pleasure, because you earned it. Happiness is the pleasure that you give to yourself when you owe yourself a moral credit, while love is the pleasure that you give to others when you owe them a moral credit for them having been a good person or having been good to you (precisely, for them having been or done something worthy of your love). If this is true, then living an ethical, moral life is the key to living a happy life.

In this way, happiness, which is pleasure given to yourself for a moral credit, is the opposite of guilt, which is pain inflicted upon yourself for a moral debt, and love, which is pleasure given to others for a credit, is the opposite of anger, which is pain inflicted upon others because of an unpaid debt. Happiness and love can be termed the positive emotions, while guilt, shame and anger are the negative emotions.

I am tempted to define another emotion, pride, and say that pride is the opposite of shame, in the sense that pride is the pleasure you feel from people seeing what a good person you are, that you reward yourself with for having impressed others with your virtue, while shame is the pain you feel when others watch you fail. However, I am resisting this temptation, because the word "pride" has many meanings, some positive and some negative: pride can mean joy in being good, or one's own knowledge and conviction that one is a good person, or joy in other people seeing oneself as good, or pleasure as reward for having done a good job, but it can also mean hubris and arrogance, or an unjustified inflated ego.

It is even true that, from the Objectivist point of view, self-knowledge of one's own virtue is the key to self-esteem, whereas virtue in the eyes and opinions of other people is a mere pretense of self-esteem (usually), so it is very ambiguous whether pride is actually virtuous or unethical, and the definition of the word is too muddy to admit of clear and precise usage. Pride, as an emotion, would merely be a type of happiness, happiness arising for a specific reason, anyway.

With respect to the seven major emotions: happiness, sadness, love, fear, guilt, shame, and anger, this leaves only fear and sadness in need of an accounting. I briefly touched upon sadness before, when discussing grief and mourning, but I will elaborate more broadly here. Sadness seems to be a biological reaction to the experience of things going wrong in your life, such as when you start crying or feel tired and apathetic, and it seems to have evolved to trigger a person to act to remove the cause of the sadness, or, at least, to notify one's friends and family so that they will try to help you.

On this analysis, sadness is similar to guilt, except that guilt is a specific reflection of you having done moral wrong, whereas sadness is precisely a reaction to things in your life going wrong, regardless of moral blameworthiness. To the extent that your guilt makes you sad, this is the emotional expression of the moral fact that having done the morally wrong thing will cause things to go wrong in your life.

The author views fear as largely a biological mechanism that evolved to make an animal flee from and run away from a threat. The only extent to which fear now matters for humans from a psychological or ethical point of view, as opposed to a biological point of view, is when the threats are social or emotional or moral, rather than a danger to survival, in which case the brain feels fear or anxiety to motivate escape.

Fear can be perfectly moral and rational if you are in a situation where running away would really be the right thing to do, such as if you have to flee from a fight you know you would lose in order to save your life, but fear can become irrational or unethical if the situation is such that you feel a need, or a desire, to escape, but the right thing to do in this situation is to face your fear, which really means, to stand up and put up a fight against whatever is threatening you.

For example, being in a new social situation where you have no friends can be scary, and might trigger social anxiety, and then you must choose whether to stay and try to talk to people and make new friends, or whether to leave because you can't stand your anxiety. The fear is your desire to flee, but what you really fear is the shame you will feel if people reject you. As such, fear itself can pose a moral test, as to whether you face your fear, or flee from it in cowardice, and this is the most common scenario where fear will possess any moral significance, as seperate and distinct from a mere biological urge to run away from physical life-threatening danger. A similar case is the person who fears starting a new job or a new career, or an athlete who fears a clutch moment in a sports game, because they fear failure, and what they truly fear is the guilt they will suffer if they fail, or the shame they will feel if other people watch them fail.

This is why, if you are practiced at the art of filing for moral bankruptcy, and you can use self-forgiveness to eliminate guilt, shame, and anger, this will also eliminate your fear of failure or your fear of rejection, because what you really fear is the guilt or shame that you will inflict upon yourself if you fail, and, with moral bankruptcy, you will no longer have to live in fear of those other negative emotions, and so you can have the ability to act, and to go after your life goals, be they friends, family, career, money, love, or whatever, without fear of feeling the pain of guilt or shame if you fail, and without fear of anger. In this way, the theory of moral bankruptcy can help you to succeed and achieve in life.

End

ABOUT THE AUTHOR

Russell Hasan

Russell Hasan is the author of these books:

NONFICTION:

A System of Legal Logic: Using Aristotle, Ayn Rand, and Analytical Philosophy to Understand the Law, Interpret Cases, and Win in Litigation (A Scholarly Monograph)

If P Then Q: Why Philosophy Can Teach You How to Think and Help You Live a Happy Life By the Methods of Applying Logic to Solve the Problems in Your Life and Achieve Success (A Scholarly Monograph)

The Power of Objectivism: Ayn Rand and John Galt and Atlas Shrugged and The Morality of Life, Intelligence, Greed, Selfishness, Rationality, Individuality, Integrity, Capitalism, Desire, and Freedom

What They Won't Tell You About Objectivism: Thoughts on the Objectivist Philosophy in the Post-Randian Era

The Apple of Knowledge: Introducing the Philosophical Scientific Method and Pure Empirical Essential Reasoning

Golden Rule Libertarianism: A Defense of Freedom in Social, Economic, and Legal Policy

On Moral Psychology and Moral Philosophy: Towards a New Theory of Emotions, Motivations, and Ethics, Using the Insight that Emotions Pay Moral Debts and Moral Credits Owed to Self and Loved Ones (also published under the alternate first edition title On Forgiveness)

XYAB Economics: A GOLD Libertarian Analysis of Money, Trade, and Freedom

A Law and Economics Approach to Litigation Costs: The Proportionality Test for E-Discovery Law (A Scholarly Monograph)

FICTION:

The Paradise Machine

The Magic Key Cards

Fallen Angel and Other Contemporary Coming-of-Age Romance Short Stories

The Golden Wand Trilogy

Project Utopia: A Libertarian Science Fiction Anthology

The Office of Heavenly Restitution: A Fantasy Fiction Anthology

The Prince, The Girl and The Revolution: A Science Fiction Fairy Tale

Rob Seablue and The Eye of Tantalus

Russell Hasan (pronouns: He, him, his) is a graduate of Vassar College and graduated with Honors from the University of Connecticut School of Law. He is a proud member of the LGBTQIA+ community and an equally proud member of the Libertarian Party. Mr. Hasan has served as a member of the LGBTQ Rights Committee of the New York City Bar Association, and has been Vice Chair of the Libertarian Party Affiliate of Fairfield County, Connecticut. He loves coffee and chewing gum, and enjoys watching sports, comedies, and science fiction/fantasy tv shows and movies. His favorite books are Atlas Shrugged and The Fountainhead and his favorite movies are Star Wars and The Matrix.

Printed in Great Britain
by Amazon

19378263R00037